CW00864863

THE OTHER SIDE
OF LUMUMBA

THE OTHER SIDE OF LUMUMBA

MY WRITINGS, ESSAYS, & HUMAN GROWTH

Michael Tombs

Copyright © 2016 by Michael Tombs.

Library of Congress Control Number:		2016900865
ISBN:	Hardcover	978-1-5144-5126-7
	Softcover	978-1-5144-5125-0
	eBook	978-1-5144-5124-3

All rights reserved. No part of this book may be reproduced or transmitted in any form or by any means, electronic or mechanical, including photocopying, recording, or by any information storage and retrieval system, without permission in writing from the copyright owner.

This is a work of fiction. Names, characters, places and incidents either are the product of the author's imagination or are used fictitiously, and any resemblance to any actual persons, living or dead, events, or locales is entirely coincidental.

Any people depicted in stock imagery provided by Thinkstock are models, and such images are being used for illustrative purposes only.
Certain stock imagery © Thinkstock.

Print information available on the last page.

Rev. date: 01/15/2016

To order additional copies of this book, contact:
Xlibris
1-888-795-4274
www.Xlibris.com
Orders@Xlibris.com
733203

Contents

DEDICATION

THIS ENTIRE BOOK is dedicated to my great grandparents, "We've come this far by faith" is rumored to be their favorite words! With a special emphasis on "tears of joy" I'm going to miss you in my lifetime…R.I.P.

December 1, 2015

ON PATRICE LUMUMBA;

"He was a foe without hate; a friend without treachery; a soldier without cruelty; a victor without oppression, and a victim without murmuring. He was a public officer without vices; a private citizen without wrong; an African without hypocrisy, and a man with deep conviction. He was a Caesar, without his ambition; Frederick, without his tyranny; Napoleon, without his selfishness, and Washington, without his reward." ~Michael Tombs

"It has often been argued is fashion art? Or is art fashion? One thing is for -sure, they are both collaborators. My story is about a situation where no one believes, but everyone believes that everyone else believes.

Ever since the murder of my brother Curtis, always in my dreams I find myself asking why do I pray and why I should go on praying. As a fully educated man I'm finished, however, as a weapon maybe I can be of some use in reference to God's will." –Michael Tombs

INTRODUCTION

THE REGINALD F. Lewis Museum of Maryland African American History & Culture is Baltimore's premier facility highlighting the history and the accomplishments of African Americans with a special focus on Maryland's African American community. A Smithsonian affiliate, the museum is the east coast's largest African American museum, occupying an 82,000 square-foot facility with ample permanent and special exhibition space, interactive learning environments, auditorium, resource center, oral history recording studio, museum shop, café, classrooms, meeting rooms, outside terrace, and reception areas. The museum is located near Baltimore's Inner Harbor at the corner of Pratt and President Street.

It was here in Mr. Lewis' museum I began to write and unravel the dreams of my father. As before mentioned in my first book "The Road Not Taken" my mother and father became my "refuge, my sanctuary, my high court" during my early years. Back in the first, days became years and years became decades, however, here I was in Mr. Lewis' museum thinking about the first democratically elected president of the Congo, Patrice Lumumba. What inspired me to reflect on this episode in America in 1961 when African American men and women were considered by most Americans as a "Negro" with limited constitutional rights and no civil rights?

I was ten years old when my father began to dramatically change. Up until my 10th birthday my father was known in my family and our community as a hard working business man. I knew him especially as a quartet singer because I had experienced many occasions listening to his quartet, The Royal Silvertones, rehearse in Jersey City, New Jersey. As I continue to reflect, my father reminded me of David Ruffin, the lead singer in the Temptations. The Temptations was popular and very successful with the Motown Sound in the 1960s.

So when my father began to listen to the Motown Sound on the radio in his car whenever I was with him, I knew his rhythm was changing. Back in the first there were 3 television stations and that was CBS, NBC, and ABC and whatever my parents listened to that's what I listened to. In addition, I knew my father's younger brother had been recently murdered by another black man in South Carolina in 1958 (who's name shall not be mentioned) however, my father was still respected by me in spite of our differences. I was just thrilled that this new music from Detroit could make me pat my feet, dance, and look at girls in a different way. I remember this one particular day in late January 1961 a news bulletin came over the radio while I was riding in the front seat of my father's car. The newsman said very clearly that Patrice Lumumba had been assassinated. I became very quiet and silent, it was the weekend, and I wanted to hear more about this man Patrice Lumumba and what other people did when someone was murdered. I knew what my family did, we went to the funeral, listened to the preacher's eulogy, and the body was put in the ground. As the radio broadcast ended I continued to be silent. We arrived at my father's store and I began my work selling candy and shining shoes. All day I thought about Patrice Lumumba and I was determined to know more about the fate this man suffered at the age of 35. I was tempted to ask my father what he knew about the other side of Lumumba however, I would wait for the right time.

PREFACE

THE RIGHT TIME never came and although Patrice Lumumba's body was never recovered or found, the murder warrant has never been served for his captors. The year was 1915 and my great grandfather, died. and 54 years later In 1969 I received my membership in The World of Islam at The Grand Mosque. The minister, Leroy Jefferson, and my friends called me Rahim Ya-Sin. The following year in 1970 my childhood and teenage girlfriend, Diane Young, called it quits. I think from age 13 to 19 we had had enough of the 1960s so we moved on. Throughout the 1970s I read the work of the great scholar and sociologist W.E.B. Du Bois, and in his Michael Brown Narrative, Du Bois passionately takes us through Brown's unsuccessful raid on Harpers Ferry, his capture, and ultimate execution. According to Du Bois Brown had several visitors in his jail cell while he awaited his final day; Brown said to one southern clergyman; "These ministers who profess to be Christians and hold slaves or advocate slavery, I cannot abide them, I will thank you to leave me alone; your prayers would be an abomination to God." To another he said, "I would not insult God by bowing down in prayer with anyone who had the blood of the slave on his skirts." And to a third who argued in favor of slavery as "a Christian institution" Michael Brown replied impatiently "My dear sir, you know nothing about Christianity; you will have to learn the A,B,C; I find you quite ignorant of what the word Christianity means… I respect you as a gentleman, of course, but it is a heathen gentleman."

When Michael Brown led a band of 21 men including "5 African Americans" and seized the federal arsenal at Harpers Ferry, Virginia in October 1859, Robert Edward Lee was given command of detachments of Maryland and Virginia Militia, soldiers, United States Marines, to suppress the uprising and arrest its leaders. By the time Lee arrived later that night, the militia on the site had surrounded Brown and his hostages. When on October 18, Brown refused the demand for surrender, Lee attacked and after 3 minutes of fighting, Brown and his followers were captured. Robert Edward Lee made a summary report of the events that took place at Harpers Ferry to Colonel Samuel Cooper, the US Army Adjutant General. According to Lee's notes, Lee believed Michael Brown was insane… "the plan (raiding Harpers Ferry Arsenal) was the attempt of a fanatic or mad man." Lee also believed that the "African Americans" used in the raid were forced to by Michael Brown himself. "The blacks, whom he (Michael Brown) forced from their homes, in this neighborhood, as far as I can learn, gave him no voluntary assistance." Lee attributed Michael Brown's "temporary success" by creating panic and confusion and by "magnifying" the number of participants involved in the raid.

ACKNOWLEDGMENTS

DECADES AFTER THE death of Dr. Martin Luther King, Jr., a curious legend developed in the Congo. Much of the rumors were true, however, history lies heavy on Africa; the long decades of colonialism, several hundred years of the Atlantic and Arab slave trade, and all too often ignored, countless centuries of indigenous slavery before that. From the colonial era, the major legacy Europe left to Africa was not democracy, it was authoritarian rule. And not as it is practiced today in countries like England, France, and The United States; On the whole continent, perhaps no nation has had a harder time than the Congo in emerging from the shadow of its past.

For example;

When independence finally came to the Congo there were fewer than thirty African university graduates in the entire territory. There were no Congolese army officers, engineers, agronomist, or physicians. The Congo had some five thousand management level positions in the civil service, only three were filled by Africans. According to Andrew Richardson, PhD, and chief research analyst for The Black Youth Organization in New York City, he reported to me that the speech by the Belgium King officially granting the Coalition government its freedom was very insulting to the newly elected Prime Minister Patrice

Lumumba. The King said; "It's now up to you gentleman to show that you are worthy of our confidence." An angry impromptu speech by Patrice Lumumba caught the world's attention. Lumumba believed that political independence was not enough to free Africa from its colonial past; the continent must also cease to be an economic colony of Europe. An inspired orator whose voice was rapidly carrying beyond his country's borders, Lumumba was a charismatic figure.

My final report came after months of research from Arthur Wedgewood, PhD, and managing supervisor to Dr. Richardson for the Lumumba case. In addition, Dr. Richardson was able to secure a much needed grant donated to my NGO "Pinnacle Holdings, LLC" by the Black Wall Street Alliance, to finalize and to complete Dr. Richardson's last report on August 21, 2014. I also suspected from many years of research papers on the ultimate death of Patrice Lumumba that several world leaders were involved in Lumumba's take down. After all, in the Congo, which is rich in copper, cobalt, diamonds, gold, tin, manganese, zinc and just barely a month earlier, an election had made Lumumba a coalition-government prime minister. His message, western governments feared, moreover, he could not be bought. Finding no sympathy in the west he asked for help from The Soviet Union. It was the first democratically elected government the Congo ever had. In substance if not form, it would be for more than thirty-five years, the last.

SUMMARY

"WHAT ULTIMATELY HAPPENED to the Congo and Patrice Lumumba in 1961 I will never really know, but I can say as a curious child of ten growing up in Newark, New Jersey I knew his death would never remain silent. Before Mobutu Sese Seko was overthrown in the Congo, in 1997, his thirty-two years in power had made him one of the world's richest men; According to Dr. Richardson & Dr. Wedgewood his personal fortune and wealth at its peak was estimated at $4 billion dollars. My hero's story has finally been researched and placed in my private papers.

The BYO's movement has finally matured in 2015 and our endowment is 100% privately funded. In addition, they have demonstrated that the power of my goals are now in their hands, and the central committee's interest is prioritized still with the people and protected by their leaders. This is a bitter sweet reflective moment in history for me as I remember and give tribute to the 100th anniversary of the passing of my great grand father."

FOREWORD

RECENTLY I VIEWED PBS moderator Gwen Ifill interview Dr. Condoleeza Rice about Ms. Rice's latest memoir "No Higher Honor." For me, history was being televised and spoken by two special women that I have come to admire, however, Dr. Rice was able to explain why her role as Secretary of State and the highest ranking African American female ever in American history during the Bush Administration (2001-2008) was so decisive. It was on August 29, 2005 when Hurricane Katrina slammed into the U.S. Gulf Coast destroying beachfront towns in Mississippi and Louisiana displacing a million people, and killing almost 1,800. When levees in New Orleans were breached, 80% of the city was submerged by the flooding. About 20% of it's 500,000 citizens were trapped in the city without power, food, or drinking water. Dr. Rice, that day, was on her way to New York City to relax and begin a much needed vacation in the Caribbean. That day Dr. Rice realized that patriotism was far more important and the epiphany forced her to realize why African American leadership was now, more than ever, important and necessary for the remainder of George Bush's Presidency. For me, the Gwen Ifill and Condoleeza Rice's interview gave closure to a sad chapter in American history and moved the conscious of America to once more believe "You are not alone". Another day has come and gone but the Ifill and Rice interview is right up there, in my opinion, with the early pioneer interviews by NBC's Gus Henningburg or PBS's Tony Brown. Maybe Ifill and Rice reminds me of Tavis Smiley and Dr. Cornell West, or maybe I relived the American Revolution through the music of Esperanza Spalding or Corinne Baily Rae...that's not my take at all. What I understand from Dr. Rice's "Memoirs" is in the words of U.S. Congressman Michael Lewis "the only way we will see those signs again will be in a book, a museum, or in a video."

THE STRANGE CASE OF OPRAH WINFREY

I N TERMS LIKE the above, the case of Oprah Winfrey goes to the drama notebooks of 2015. Oprah shocked early generations of critics. I knew much better, Oprah was just simply ahead of her time. We all were students of the Civil Rights age as well as the 1960s era. I loved a rebel. How could I condemn Oprah, how could I condemn a woman inspired by work, hunger for power, beauty, and heroic achievement... even though her concept of these things is bourgeois and romantic? I personally believe that "Romantic love will be the last delusion of the old order." As I reflect on 2015, Oprah took courage, in my opinion, to challenge and interview all the guest on her TV show. Now, in the Age of Barak Obama, one might reasonably ask, how would Oprah have dealt with "The War on Terror" or dropping the bomb on Hiroshima. That alone, would be reason enough to take another look at Oprah and see what she envies in men's power, and by being herself an African American daughter she can see the yearning for power over another's life comes out of a sense of powerlessness to control her own. I see that she is temperamentally suited to play her socially assigned role and that it is society not academia, which traps her. A women's liberation emphasis would by no means bring out all the dramatic possibilities on Oprah's new cable network, however, this is why it is so disappointing for me to see actors such as Vanessa Williams, Halle Berry, Tyra Banks, and Toni Braxton's current portrayal as women with a Ladies Home Journal of "New York City" problems not expressing a wider flamboyant dimension, and in my opinion there is no passion or power or the real potential I observe in stars such as Beyoncé Knowels, Mariah Carey, Ashanti Douglas, and Alicia Keys. They all play a great soap opera, but that is not the creation of my complex mind. Is this what defeat looks like? Furthermore, in my opinion, Oprah is a grown woman now and she's not terrified of scandal like Kim Kardashian or Karrinne Stephans because she has much too much to hide or worry about unloving, foolish, dangerous men and woman speaking about Freedom, Beauty, or Nobility. Should we forgive them, for they know not what they do? In my opinion Oprah is a golden goddess "Fire" in our living and bedrooms. In my opinion this is closer to African American comedy, rather than African American tragedy, and in my opinion the pantheon of American warriors (past and present) will forever and never cease to be my enlightenment when it comes to the empirical questions and answers of American justice "No threat standing." It is simply "the way we were."

KINGS OF THE COURT

M ICHAEL TOMBS IS an African American psychotherapist and Naturopath ND of African American descent. My theories questioned some traditional Psychotherapy views, particularly the theory of sexuality, as well as the instinct orientation of psychotherapy and its genetic psychology. As such I'm often classified as Neo-Freudian. I look at neurosis in a different light from other psychotherapist of my time in 2015. My expansive interest in the subject led me to compile a detailed theory of neurosis, with data from both my clients and patients. I believe neurosis to be a continued process, with neuroses commonly occurring sporadically in one's lifetime. This is in contrast to the opinions of my contemporaries who believe neurosis is, like more severe mental conditions, a negative malfunction of the mind in response to external stimuli, such as bereavement, divorce or negative experiences during childhood and adolescence...

I believe these assumptions to be less important, except for influences during childhood. Rather, I place significant emphasis on parental indifferences towards the child, believing that a child's perception of events, as opposed to the parent's intentions, is the key to understanding a person's neurosis. For instance, a child might feel a lack of warmth and affection should a parent make fun of the child's feelings – thereby underestimating the significance of the child's state. The parent may also casually neglect to fulfill promises, which in turn could have effect on the child's mental state. Strongly opinionated, and demanding loyalty from my followers, I established a highly influential training program in the BYO. I am considered one of the founding members of the BYO. My theoretical work gradually centered on a speculative hypothesis eventually accepted by Cliff Carter, which stated that life may be a fragile occurrence, that it is drawn towards an inorganic state, and therefore, in an unspecified sense, contains a drive towards death. In psychological terms Eros (properly, the life instinct) the postulated sustaining and uniting principle of life, is thereby presumed to have a companion force, Thanatos (death instinct), which allegedly seeks to terminate and disintegrate life. Both Carter and myself regarded these biomental forces, discovered by Ibn Al-Nafis as the foundations of the psyche. These were human instincts ("Triebe") unrelated to the animal instincts of ethology.

THE EQUALIZER

MY FAMILY LEGACY starts from slavery to CEO. I was sitting in my condo on East 94th Street in Manhattan checking out my website, facebook, twitter, and business accounts on my mac and I-Pad when suddenly my I-Phone started ringing. It was my girlfriend, Tabitha Franklin, downstairs in the car waiting for me to come down to head over to her condo on Lexington Avenue in Manhattan. Tabitha was educated in Canada, born in London, and now living in Manhattan as a NYU medical student. Her plan is to practice medicine in sunny California, while her mother, an attorney, owned the family horse ranch in Oklahoma. In the interim, her father, an Indian diplomat, would pay for her condo in NYC. I have always been attracted to powerful women in my early years in Manhattan. When Condoleeza Rice was appointed National Security Advisor to George Bush and later confirmed as US Secretary of State I was amazed. But that was short lived when Hillary Clinton was confirmed under Barak Obama and I thought the job will go to UN Ambassador to the United States, Susan Rice. We now live in The Age of President Barak Obama, a time when Apple is moving to become the first Trillion Dollar company in market value in the history of the world. As I reflect on my last vacation in Columbia, South Carolina; My Great Grand Father has departed from us, and my Great Grand Mother has departed from us. My Grand Mother, Grand Father and their sons, has departed from us. The last surviving member of my parent's clan is my mother. It always seemed sad that after 9 decades my mother never corrected the spelling of her name. In fact, my mother never even voted in the United States national elections for any candidate until the late 1970s. She never could or would admit the imposition of "Jim Crow" and segregation. The social afflictions of slavery that DuBois confronted were real. One such reference I do have is the powerful story of Frederick Douglas. Douglas was born a slave to become a United States diplomat and during his post slavery struggle he was able to observe and write these words 114 years ago; "Though the colored man is no longer subject to barter and sale he is surrounded by an adverse settlement which fetters all his movements. In his downward course he meets with no resistance, but his course upward is resented and resisted at every step of his...progress. If he comes in ignorance, rags and wretchedness he conforms to the popular belief of his character, and in that character he is welcome; but if he shall come as a gentleman, a scholar and a statesman, he is hailed as a contradiction to the national faith concerning his race, and his coming is resented as impudence. In one case he may provoke contempt and derision, but in the other he is an affront to pride and provokes malice." ~ Frederick Douglas

WHY PINNACLE HOLDINGS, LLC

IN MY OPINION, if the student is not an expert in Anthropology and Archeology, it might appear that there are no essential methodological differences between the two. I believe for several reasons the connection exist. I first considered the "Empirical Reality" point of view. Scientist in both fields attempt to discuss laws of acceptability for a circumscribed group of phenomena in order to make the interconnection of these phenomena as clearly and understandable as possible.

For example,

Historic tradition is in every society, and no where have we overcome what I call 'the predatory phase" of human development. The observable archeological facts belong to this phase, and even new laws that evolve are not applicable to other phases. In my opinion, the real purpose of education is to overcome and move beyond the predatory phase of human development. Anthropology gives us answers of a precise and ethical end. Let me describe my personal experience, and why I began to research my Narrative for the sequel to the "The Road Not Taken." Recently I was on the Amtrak travelling from Manhattan to Washington, D.C. and the man in the next seat was born and raised in Virginia, had a PhD in Anthropology. In addition, he just started teaching archeology at a major university in the south. This intelligent young professor began to explain to me the difficulty he was having in finding archeological sites to excavate with his students. The professor was interested in my advice…My answer to the professor was, "it is easy to raise questions, but difficult to answer them without a reasonable approach." I further advised that he should develop his own cosmology that would influence the student through his own rigid conduct. Modern Anthropology has taught us, through research and investigation, of primitive cultures, that the behavior of human beings differ greatly, however, the whole life process of ants and bees is fixed all the way down to the smallest detail by instincts. Man, on the other hand acquires at birth, through heredity, a genetic constitution which is fixed. In addition, man and woman acquires a cultural constitution they adopt from society through communication. Memory; the ability to make new combinations and the gift of oral communication have made developments which are not dictated by biology. These developments manifest themselves in institutions, organizations, literature, scientific and engineering technologies, and works of art. I then made a comment of fact to the young professor by reflecting on his own home state of Virginia; President Abraham Lincoln ordered his commanding General Ulysses S. Grant to begin the burning of most southern capitals and many southern cities in the 1860s as a goal to bring a military end to the American Civil War. This explains how it happens that, it is this cultural constitution in man and woman, that with the passage of time, is subject to change and can determine the relationship between the individual and society. Science, however, cannot create ends, and certainly cannot instill them in human beings. Medical science can teach the student to reach specific ends, but the ends themselves are discovered by personalities with both ethical and political science ideals. This can determine, in my opinion, the slow evolution of society.

MY WRITINGS, ESSAYS, & HUMAN GROWTH...

"Contemporary man is blind to the fact that, with all his rationality and efficiency, he is possessed by "powers" that are beyond his control. His gods and demons have not disappeared at all; they have merely got new names. They keep him on the run with restlessness, vague apprehensions, psychological complications, an insatiable need for pills, alcohol, tobacco, food...and, above all, a large array of neuroses." ~ Carl Jung

WHEN I WAS a young boy I wanted to complete my elementary education at a military academy in New Jersey and afterwards enlist in The United States Armed Forces as a medical doctor. This spontaneous feeling continued in my early environment until I was ten. My father was made aware of my intentions by my 4th grade teacher and shortly after my father's conversation with my teacher he took my brother and I on a vacation to Columbia, South Carolina to visit my grandmother's estate.

My brother Curtis and I often wondered why my father waited until I was an adult to introduce me to Curtis's mother "Gloria." But in Newark, New Jersey that was his house and he made the rules and regulations. My father was my first hero, and no man has ever made me feel so needed, so wanted, and so insecure. It is simply the way he wanted to be honored. My father had six children, myself and three sisters born to my mother. In addition he was the genetic father of Curtis born to his mother "Gloria." After the visit to my grandmother's home in Columbia, South Carolina I was told by my father that I would not be attending military school and that I should choose another career path. That was not to be because as Curtis and I grew older into our early twenties we began to have similar Islamic religious beliefs. One day while hanging out in the hood we met an old Muslim griot named Ahmad, and he invited Curtis and I to a local Muslim restaurant in the neighborhood. We were very curious to know why Ahmad always lectured us about Heaven, and what he knew about Heaven.

After ordering our lunch, Ahmad said, "when we arrive in heaven we would be directed to an orientation seminar where the authorities explained the local rules". To our surprise, we learned that right-wing religious groups were essentially correct, and family values were indeed a cornerstone of our new environment. The authorities had long established a traditional family structure premised on separation of generations and the stability of marriages; a top would always marry a bottom, a charmer would always mate with a strange bird, and an uptown girl would always marry a downtown cool cat. Curtis and I were satisfied with the arrangement. But we learned later from Ahmad that the social structure in heaven had not always been so secure. Originally, dangerous infiltrators had threatened the hierarchical foundation of society. In Heaven, however, most problems can be solved. God had sent a personal guardian angel, and the angels and their charges had heroically worked together to avert the threat to the hierarchy and preserve the ordered society that we would enjoy. Even so, Heaven was not entirely safe. The angels turned out to be free agents, with no contract binding them to a single generation. The angels, who had rescued the hierarchy, now threatened to destroy Heaven's family values. Curtis and I became very upset, however, despite Heaven's well advertised attractions we were finding it a surprisingly stressful place to live.

MY EARLY YEARS AND LIFE IN MANHATTAN

"We made too many speeches and did not do the necessary work; the unglamorous off camera work that would have made it possible, that was our great mistake, ceremony that lacked substance." ~Michael Henrik Clark

MICHAEL TOMBS STARTED his career at Waverly County College as a student and Gear Up Newark adviser in 1968. Since then I've progressed along the administrative career ladder from associate degree to corporation president and now CEO of King Enterprises, Inc., I have served as interim President of Pinnacle Holdings, LLC for 4 years. My responsibilities include administrative oversight and instructional leadership for my Wall Street partners that serves over 10,000 clients from 119 countries with a wide variety of programs: adult financial literacy, high school completion, English for speakers of other languages, associate arts and sciences degrees, career certificates and continuing workforce education instruction. Additionally, this year in 2015 my executive staff applied for membership in the first Screen Actors Guild (SAG) cable TV broadcasting school based in the Tri-State area in the State of New York. I earned a bachelor's/ undergraduate degree in anatomy & physiology (Biology) from the University of Medicine & Dentistry in Newark, NJ, a masters and ND Doctor degree from the University of Bridgeport in Connecticut. I hold a Certificate in Banking and Finance of Lifelong Education from Waverly County College and was a BYO Senior Fellow with the League for Innovation at WCC. I have been very committed to community, state, and national leadership in areas for which I hold great passion and insight. In 2000, I chaired the Newark Community Council's study on cable TV broadcasting and its impact on economic development. I was inducted into the BYO's Community Educators Hall of Fame in recognition of my statewide leadership and support of adult education and workforce development. I have served on numerous Manhattan associations and advisory councils, including membership in The New Jersey Historical Society. In 2006, I launched my name brand "Rose Street Entertainment." In 2015, I'll travel to St. Thomas, USVI to serve as the principle underwriter for my new TV miniseries. Additionally, I now serve on the Board of Trustees for Pinnacle Holdings, LLC in Manhattan.

THE LEGACY OF GENERATION X

Reorganizing BYO (The Black Youth Organization)

> "History is not a bedtime story. It is a comprehensive engagement with often obscure documents and books no longer read, books shelved in old archives, and fragile pamphlets contemporaneous with the subject under study, all of which reflect a world view not ours. We cannot make the 1960s African American men and women of Newark, New Jersey 'familiar" by endowing them and their families with the emotions we prefer to universalize;"

For example;

IN 'A HISTORY Of Reading' Steven Fischer explains that "Today's white-collar worker spends more time reading than eating, drinking, grooming, travelling, socializing or on general entertainment and sport - that is, five to eight hours of each working day. (Only sleep appears to claim as much time.) The computer and internet? Both are reading revolutions."

He continues to explain;"...Each human being, according to his innate capacity, learns something as the days go on. He accumulates experience, to some extent he correlates it and interprets it. He becomes wiser as the years pass. And then he or she dies; and the complex neural mechanism, developed and refined so laboriously, disintegrates into dust. In primitive society, something of the gathered wisdom is passed on by word of mouth."

For example;

Of all mankind's manifold creations, "wrote Guy Deutscher" language must take pride of place. Other inventions, the wheel, agriculture, sliced bread, may have transformed our material existence, but the advent of language is what made us human. Compared to language, all other inventions pale in significance, since everything we have ever achieved depends on language and originates from it. Without language, we could never have embarked on our ascent to unparalleled power over all other animals, and even over nature itself..."

"First they came for the communist, but I was not a communist so I did not speak out. Then they came for the Socialist, but I was not a Socialist so I did not speak out, then they came for the Trade Unionist, but I was not a Trade Unionist so I did not speak out. Then they came for the Jews, but I was not a Jew so I did not speak out. And when they came for me, there was no one left to speak out for me."- Martin Niemoller

"I've read the adventures of Superman, Batman, Sky Fall, Star Wars, Billy Elliott, and Harry Potter in my later years, however, when I became 18 years old in 1968 the United States Government required all young men of age to register for the military draft. My appointment letter to report to the draft board was not an easy demand to accept. When asked by the draft board officer "what would I do if I was drafted into the United States Military" my answer was "I would organize the soldiers to fight against the real criminals." That answer prompted the draft board officer to classify me as 1Y (undesirable to serve). My activities in my community during the 1960s were about organizing young students to participate in civil disobedience. I knew my activities were being watched and recorded and the draft board interview confirmed my suspicions. The war in Viet Nam claimed 68 thousand lives in the United States Military before defeat by the Viet Cong became a reality to the United States government in Washington, D.C. and the Pentagon in Virginia. In my later years I immediately began to read books and letters about certain men and women who had or possessed, in my opinion, important and certain information".

THE 3 TRANSIT LETTERS

1)

HOWARD ROBARD HUGHES Jr., born on December 24, 1905, in Houston, is largely known for being one of the wealthiest men and one of the most famous recluses, but Hughes had many professional accomplishments before withdrawing from public life.

Son of a successful oil-drill tool manufacturer, Howard inherited the family business in 1923 at the age of 18. He used some of his fortune to finance films, beginning in 1926. Howard produced several movies, including the World War I epic *Hell's Angels* (1930), which featured expensive aerial fight sequences and a then-unknown actress named Jean Harlow. Some of his other significant films were *Scarface* (1932) and *The Outlaw* (1941). During his days in Hollywood, Howard developed a reputation for being a playboy, dating such actresses as Katharine Hepburn, Ava Gardner and Ginger Rogers.

Howard developed a passion for flying and founded his own aircraft company in the early 1930s. Besides designing and building planes, he risked his own life several times testing planes and setting world air-speed records in the mid- to late 1930s. While he is credited with many aviation innovations, such as the first retractable landing gear, he is also remembered for one of his biggest flops–the H-4 Hercules, which the press nicknamed the Spruce Goose. Hughes labored on this oversized wooden seaplane for years, finishing it in 1947. It was flown only once.

Howard died on April 5, 1976. After his death, numerous fake versions of his will surfaced, leading to a battle over his fortune.

2)
Reginald F. Lewis

Reginald F. Lewis (December 7, 1942 – January 19, 1993) was an American businessman. He was the richest African-American man in the 1980s. Born in Baltimore, Maryland, he grew up in a middle-class neighborhood. He won a football scholarship to Virginia State College, graduating with a degree in economics in 1965. He graduated from Harvard Law School in 1968.

In 1992, *Forbes* listed Lewis among the 400 richest Americans, with a net worth estimated at $400 million. He also was the first African American to build a billion dollar company, Beatrice Foods.

In 1987, Lewis bought Beatrice International Foods from Beatrice Companies for $985 million, renaming it TLC Beatrice International, a snack food, beverage, and grocery store conglomerate that was the largest African-American owned and managed business in the U.S. The deal was partly financed through Mike Milken of the maverick investment bank Drexel Burnham Lambert. In order to reduce the amount needed to finance the LBO, Lewis came up with a plan to sell off some of the division's assets simultaneous with the takeover.

When TLC Beatrice reported revenue of $1.8 billion in 1987, it became the first black-owned company to have more than $1 billion in annual sales. At its peak in 1996, TLC Beatrice International Holdings Inc. had sales of $2.2 billion and was number 512 on Fortune magazine's list of 1,000 largest companies.

In 1987 Lewis established The Reginald F. Lewis Foundation, which funded grants of approximately $10 million to various non-profit programs and organizations while he was alive. His first major grant was an unsolicited $1 million to Howard University in 1988; the federal government matched the grant, making the gift to Howard University $2 million, which was used to fund an endowment for scholarships, fellowships, and faculty sabbaticals. In 1992, he donated $3 million to Harvard Law School, the largest grant at the time in the law school's history. In gratitude, the school renamed its International Law Center the Reginald F. Lewis International Law Center, the first major facility at Harvard named in honor of an African-American. Reginald Lewis was married to Loida Nicolas-Lewis. He died at age 50, from brain cancer.

3)
Ibn Saud

Full Name;
Abdulaziz ibn Abdul Rahman ibn Faisal ibn Turki ibn Abdullah ibn Muhammad Al Saud, usually known within the Arab world as Abdulaziz and usually known outside the Arab world as Ibn Saud, was the first monarch and founder of Saudi Arabia and the House of Saud.

He reconquered his family's ancestral home city of Riyadh in 1902, starting three decades of conquests that made him the ruler of nearly all of central Arabia. He consolidated his control over the Najd in 1922, then conquered the Hejaz in 1925. He extended his dominions into the Kingdom of Saudi Arabia in 1932. As King, he presided over the discovery of petroleum in Saudi Arabia in 1938 and the beginning of large-scale oil production after World War II. His kingdom took off like a rocket. He fathered many children, including 45 sons, "and all of the subsequent kings of Saudi Arabia." In 1925, the forces of Ibn Saud captured the holy city of Mecca from Sharif Hussein, ending 700 years of Hashemite rule. On 8 January 1926, the leading figures in Mecca, Madina and Jeddah proclaimed Ibn Saud the King of Hejaz. On 20 May 1927, the British government signed the Treaty of Jeddah, which abolished the Darin protection agreement and recognized the independence of the Hejaz and Najd with Ibn Saud as its ruler. Ibn Saud had to first eliminate the right of his own father in order to rule, and then distance and contain the ambitions of his five brothers – particularly his oldest brother Muhammad who fought with him during the battles and conquests that had given birth to the state. In accordance with the customs of his people, Abdul Aziz headed a polygamous household comprising several wives and concubines. According to some sources, he had twenty-two consorts. Many of his marriages were contracted in order to cement alliances with other clans, during the period when the Saudi state was founded and stabilized. Abdul Aziz was the father of almost a hundred children, including forty-five sons.

In October 1953, Ibn Saud was seriously ill due to heart disease. He died in his sleep of a heart attack at the palace of Prince Faisal in Ta'if on 9 November 1953 (2 Rabī□ al-Awwal 1373 AH) at the age of 78. Prince Faisal was at his side. Funeral prayer was performed at Al Hawiya in Ta'if. His body was brought to Riyadh where he was buried in Al Oud cemetery.

MY TRIBUTE TO
IMAM ALI RASHID,
AMERICAN MUSLIM

ANGELA BIKO WALKED into my life in December 1986 in Sparta, New Jersey. I now clearly remember our history because my father, Michael Tombs Sr., had died in September 1986 of a heart attack and my mother asked me to run the family business in the townships of Millburn and Frenchtown, New Jersey. Angela and I began to communicate when she stopped by my store every day on her way to work. I was still in the grieving process of the sudden loss of my father's death and Angela was very sensitive to my loss. Angela commuted by train from East Orange, New Jersey to my store at the Millburn train station in Millburn, New Jersey. Instantly we became good friends, exchanged phone numbers, and very soon began to date. Our romance began to become rather serious very quickly in early 1987. In June 1987 we were engaged to be married and we both were fully aware that I was a devout Muslim and she was a practicing Hebrew Israelite. The sudden romance between

Angela and I caught me off guard and prompted me to request a private audience with the Muslim Imam Ali Rashid in his Manhattan office at 102 West 116th Street at Masjid Malcolm Shabazz in reference to our marriage plans. My fiancé & I arrived on time and the Imam began to discuss the pros, cons, and our budget. I then began to explain that we had agreed to hold the reception in the famous "Cotton Club" in Harlem. Suddenly the Imam blurted out "who's going to marry you?" My answer was "you" and the Imam said "okay I was just wondering". We all laughed and I requested another appointment to discuss my immediate plans. The Imam then scheduled we should return the following week. Angela and I never returned, we decided to elope because it would be financially more prudent. I immediately called the Imam to inform him of our immediate plans and he wished my fiancé and I well. Years later after Sheila "Tia" Tombs, Beverley Lancaster, & Laureen Gordon had died and passed on, I realized that I had been played by Angela Biko like a French violin… it was another epiphany for me as I was developing a more clear understanding and pure interpretation of the "Abrahamic Faiths."

On February 25, 1975, Nation of Islam leader, the Honorable Elijah Muhammad, died and was succeeded by his son Imam W. D. Mohammed. Imam W. Deen Mohammed brought the true religious teachings of al-Islam to the community and to the larger American society. Embracing all of humanity in its fold, the concept of al-Islam as the religion of peace captivated huge segments of the American public and indeed the world took notice of the *World Community of Islam in the West* as Imam W. D. Mohammed initially named the new "strained" Islamic community which emerged from the Nation of Islam. In 1976, Imam W. D. Mohammed renamed Muhammad's Temple of Islam #7 at 102 West 116th Street as Masjid Malcolm Shabazz in honor of the powerful and far reaching contributions of Malcolm X to America, the establishment of al Islam in the United States and to the cause of Universal Human Rights. From 1976 to January 1993, Imam Ali Rashid from California presided over the new ground breaking educational and spiritual community dimension of Imam W. D. Mohammad's new mission at Masjid Malcolm Shabazz. Imam Ali Rashid, the leader of the Malcolm Shabazz Masjid in Harlem was born in Los Angeles, California. In addition, Imam Rashid attended college at the University of Oregon and graduated from the California State University system in the late 1940's. After moving to New York in 1975 to become leader of the Harlem mosque, he earned a master's degree in education from the City University of New York in 1983. Imam Rashid served in the United States Army in the late 40's. He converted to Islam in 1952 and joined the Nation of Islam…R.I.P.

THE KILLER ANGEL

THE PHRASES "LORD of the east and the west, lord of the believers and the disbelievers, lord of men's necks, and Rahim the magnificent" has become idioms about logical fallacies. A fallacy is an argument that uses poor reasoning. An argument can be fallacious whether or not its conclusion is true. A fallacy can be either formal or informal. An error that stem from a poor logical form is sometimes called a formal fallacy or simply an invalid argument. An informal fallacy is an error in reasoning that does not originate in improper logical form. Arguments committing informal fallacies may be formally valid, but still fallacious. Fallacies of presumption fail to prove the conclusion by assuming the conclusion in the proof. Fallacies of weak inference fail to prove the conclusion with insufficient evidence. Fallacies of distraction fail to prove the conclusion with irrelevant evidence, like emotion. Fallacies of ambiguity fail to prove the conclusion due to vagueness in words, phrases, or grammar.

For example;
In social psychology pluristic ignorance is a situation where the majority of group members privately reject a norm, but assume incorrectly that most others accept it, also described as, 'no one believes, but everyone thinks that everyone believes." In short, pluristic ignorance

is a bias about a social group, held by a social group. Lack of public opposition then helps perpetuate a norm that may be, in fact, disliked by most people. A lot of people are wrong about something but because everyone sees this wrong idea as the perceived social norm, no one speaks up against it. Pluristis ignorance can also be contrasted with the false consensus effect. In pluristic ignorance, people privately disdain but publicly support a norm (or a belief), while the false consensus effect causes people to wrongly assume that most people think like they do, while in reality most people do not think like they do (and express the disagreement openly).

For instance, pluristic ignorance may lead a student to drink alcohol excessively because he or she believes that everyone else does that, while in reality everyone else also wishes they could avoid binge drinking, but no one expresses that due to fear of being ostracized. A false consensus for the same situation would mean that the student believes that most other people do enjoy that and openly express their opinion about it.

1961

MICHAEL TOMBS

Other names: Rahim Ya-Sin, Abdul Rahim

"I had no clue and heard no more reports about the death of Patrice Lumumba…"

I AM NOW an African American businessman and the father of numerous children with five different women. I am the founder of King Enterprises, Inc. and instrumental in developing, Rose Street Entertainment Agency, and Pinnacle Holdings, LLC (my product line).

As before mentioned, when I was eleven years old, my father, said to me that I would not be attending military school. My dreams of becoming a doctor in the United States Marine Corp suddenly set me on a course in unchartered waters. I was like a duck in the water that was hit over the head. I am not exactly clear as to when I started earning money, however, I can't remember not having my own money.

1962

THE MONKEY THAT GOT AWAY

"I had no clue and heard no more reports about the death of Patrice Lumumba…"

B
Y THE EARLY 1960s I had met all 5 of my contemporary friends including my brother Curtis. At some point in the mid 1960s we all started working and immediately saw the potential in putting our money together to purchase clothes and suits to go out on dates with our favorite girlfriends. The more money I earned, my mother opened a savings account for me at the Howard Savings Bank in Newark, New Jersey. The more I earned and saved, the more I began to travel to Harlem and visit my cousin Sekou Sundiatta. Over the next few years, I started asking my friends if they wanted to go to Harlem and hang out with me, my cousins, and my girlfriends who lived in East Harlem. My brother Curtis, my capos, and my friends never really clicked with my Harlem friends because they were in love with the girls in Newark, so they began going over to Harlem with me only if we were going over to smoke some weed or sniff a little coke.

1963

THE NIGHT I FELL IN LOVE

"I had no clue and heard no more reports about the death of Patrice Lumumba…"

CATHERINE JACOBS WALKED into my life at West Kinney Jr. High School. When our eyes met in the school hallway I immediately became attracted to her. To me she was built the right way and from what I saw she had the right attitude. I was in the 7th grade and Catherine Jacobs was in the 8th grade so I foolishly thought that I had 2 years to get to know her because our school went up to the 9th grade and then we all would transfer on to high school. Right after the Christmas and New Year holidays of 1964, Catherine didn't return to school in January 1964. I panicked, I began going to her classes and no one knew where she was. I couldn't ask my new girlfriend, Diane Young, because she would know what I was up to. My classmates who lived in Catherine's neighborhood did in fact report that they did see her regularly, however, I didn't know where she lived. Several months later one Sunday morning in the Spring

I was walking to my family's church on West Kinney Street in Newark, New Jersey. I loved walking alone to the New Salem Baptist Church in the early mornings because I could slide over to Diane's house to see if she was hanging around outside her building on Mercer Street. Suddenly I heard a familiar female voice from a 2nd floor window across the street calling down to someone just below her window. I looked up to focus on the familiar voice and noticed it was Catherine Jacobs speaking from a second floor window to a young woman she knew standing below her window. I now knew where she lived, but she was pregnant! She still looked gorgeous, however, I was only thirteen years old and was in no way going to continue being in love with a pregnant woman. I didn't know what to think next. I was never to see her again until she registered in my high school in January 1968. We both graduated from South Side High School in the same class together and remained close, however, my secret infatuation never interfered with my education. I still question my observations and motives as a young man, however, I just convinced myself then that Catherine Jacobs knew that I was in love with her and it was all just a part of growing up in my world.

1964

UNION STATION AND HELL'S KITCHEN

I had no clue and heard no more reports about the death of
Patrice Lumumba…

T HE PENDULUM AGAINST
racism in 2015 is extremely strong
in the African American community and their economic plans to destroy
racism plays out in an odd altruism such as equal employment, equal
housing, and the grand prize…The U.S. Presidency of Barak Obama.
America is not weak because there is a lack of patriotism, America is
weak, in my opinion, because economic opportunity is low and the
creation of an employment plan cannot sustain popular enthusiasm
and many African Americans believe that the uncle toms, men and
women, and the majority of Americas politicians has sold black people
down the river and rides the backs of middle and upper class whites out
into the middle of the Atlantic Ocean, Pacific Ocean, or the Gulf Coast
with the crushing "debt ceiling" controlled by Washington politics thus

encouraging their society to be color blind to national, state, and local leadership.

What I know for sure about racism is that it is a narrow philosophy that only grows out of frustration when ignorance, weak men and women's ideas, are not exposed during economic decline in America's cities and states. What are some of the problems of an underdeveloped economy? In my opinion you have job loss, under educated men and women, and mental illness. The criminal justice and prison system is a symptom of this crisis, however, historic solutions has been eclipsed by Globalization. The Road Not Taken means more money and more problems. Americas GNP is no longer depending on millions; America's recovery depends on trillions of dollars.

1965

I had no clue and heard no more reports about the death of Patrice Lumumba...

Dead Men Laughing
Lumumba's Last Letter
Written to His Wife Just Before His Death

My dear companion,

"I WRITE YOU these words without knowing if they will reach you, when they will reach you, or if I will still be living when you read them. All during the length of my fight for the independence of my country, I have never doubted for a single instant the final triumph of the sacred cause to which my companions and myself have consecrated our lives. But what we wish for our country, its right to an honorable life, to a spotless dignity, to an independence without restrictions, Belgian colonialism and its Western allies-who have found direct and indirect support, deliberate and not deliberate among certain high officials of the United Nations, this organization in which we placed all our confidence when we called for their assistance-have not wished it.

They have corrupted certain of our fellow countrymen, they have contributed to distorting the truth and our enemies, that they will rise up like a single person to say no to a degrading and shameful colonialism and to reassume their dignity under a pure sun.

We are not alone. Africa, Asia, and free and liberated people from every corner of the world will always be found at the side of the Congolese. They will not abandon the light until the day comes when there are no more colonizers and their mercenaries in our country. To my children whom I leave and whom perhaps I will see no more, I wish that they be told that the future of the Congo is beautiful and that it expects for each Congolese, to accomplish the sacred task of reconstruction of our independence and our sovereignty; for without dignity there is no liberty, without justice there is no dignity, and without independence there are no free men.

No brutality, mistreatment, or torture has ever forced me to ask for grace, for I prefer to die with my head high, my faith steadfast, and my confidence profound in the destiny of my country, rather than to live in submission and scorn of sacred principles. History will one day have its say, but it will not be the history that Brussels, Paris, Washington or the United Nations will teach, but that which they will teach in the countries emancipated from colonialism and its puppets. Africa will write its own history, and it will be, to the north and to the south of the Sahara, a history of glory and dignity.

Do not weep for me, my dear companion. I know that my country, which suffers so much, will know how to defend its independence and its liberty. Long live the Congo! Long live Africa!"

1966

PATRICE

"I had no clue and heard no more reports about the death of Patrice Lumumba…"

The End of the Road

CONSTANCE MILLS WALKED into my life at South Side High School. In my mind she was the most beautiful woman I had ever seen since I graduated from Jr. High school in June 1965. I hadn't seen Catherine Jacobs in years, however, I did dream about her from time to time. Constance Mills was not very different, she too was a junior at South Side High School and I was a sophomore at South Side High. She dressed fabulous, her hair was always just right, and she always looked hot and gorgeous. It took me almost six months just to introduce myself. By then I knew she knew what I was up to because I couldn't take my eyes off her as she moved back and forth to her locker in the school hallways, so I just played it cool and stepped up my game by having hooky parties with my favorite sex interest. In June 1967 Constance graduated from South Side and I was never to see her again. I had many girlfriends as a teenager, however Catherine Jacobs and Constance Mills, for me in my mind I believe was love at first sight. I began to visit Harlem more often, in fact, I would go over alone most of the time on the weekends or the days I wasn't working. One day Sekou Sundiatta took me over to my Aunt Jennifer's house over on West 118th Street close to the Apollo uptown in Harlem. Jennifer was my grandmother's sister. My genetic grandmother, Eloise Graham, passed away when my mother was very young (the rumor was, my mother was two years old) and my grandfather, Michael McClain, remarried Melanie . That's how we became family. Aunt Jennifer also had a son named Curtis, same first name as my brother. This particular day Curtis was very secretive. He had a package that he wanted to give to Sekou so they went into Curtis's room to talk. I didn't think too much about it at the time, but as the weeks and months went by Curtis began to lose weight and so did Sekou. I thought they were just getting high too much. But then Curtis kept wearing the same clothes, he had a strange odor, and his complexion began to get darker. Curtis was always a light skinned dude but his voice was very country and his voice stood out in Harlem unlike Sekou's deep baritone Harlem voice. One day Sekou told me that the word from Curtis is that Bumpy Michaelson's people had promised him a new package and all their troubles would be over. I immediately relayed the message to my brother Curtis and my crew and they were all put on standby based on drugs that we all had previously tested and enjoyed very much. The news was received extremely well in my neighborhood in Newark so I had no need to doubt my cousin Sekou's word. After all, my crew had visited Sekou's home several times and I had broke several of my girlfriends and east side shorties off in his bed room. This new business deal, at the time, was a learning curve, however, I would play my last desperate card if it meant that I would get out of the ghetto or living in the "Little Bricks" in Newark. It was time, high time, for Harlem to make good on its word. When I was young man I visited my first cousin Porsha and her husband Sidney over on 8th avenue and Adam Clayton Powell Blvd.. I used to play downstairs in the early mornings alone in the "big field" right across the street from Lenox Terrace. It was exciting and the park seemed so large. I would get up early in the mornings when my younger cousins, Gracella, Sheila,

Sandra, and Angela were all asleep just to go down and play on the swings in the big park, however, I missed my male cousins and the east side boys in Harlem. I missed being on the 18th floor at 106th Street and looking out at the cruise ships beautiful yachts, and boats on the mighty east river.

1967

"I had no clue and heard no more reports about the death of Patrice Lumumba…"

New Edition

MY SUMMARY REPORT that I will deliver to the BYO at our next annual meeting in St. Thomas, USVI (December 2015) will focus specifically on Patrice Lumumba as a man, a soldier, and the events that destroyed his political and military career. The wounds Lumumba suffered would have certainly killed him. After intense research Dr. Richardson and Dr. Wedgewood emerged with a spirit that would make my organization and America proud. The BYO has started the educational process, the work, and eventually young interns will be invited to be liberated from the "I can't do" attitude to the "yes we can movement" and education will ultimately express an appreciation of the rise and the fall of Lumumba's movement and the causes that evolved from colonization. The decision will come down to one of two choices, economics or a continuance of the Congo's African status. In my opinion, on that violent and terrible night in 1961, the forces and enemies of Lumumba won and Patrice Lumumba moved on with his life. It is an honor to hear the great news that this man's family has received from history's intellectuals and realist. And I really don't care to hear if Brittany Spears is engaged, Kim Kardashian is divorced, or Beyonce is pregnant. What matters to me is that I became a man because an intervention was made in my young life, and one night in Manhattan my experiences would lead me to believe that an African could win a contest and did as far as I was concerned...God bless you Patrice Lumumba!

1968

"I had no clue and heard no more reports about the death of
Patrice Lumumba…"

Boys to Men

ALTHOUGH I HAD come to the
end of my conscious search for
Patrice Lumumba, 1968 came and went, however, the student protest
movement that the BYO had set in motion in Newark, New Jersey was
going strong. There were two things that I was determined to do, and
that was have many girlfriends and have a lot of sex. The Rev. Dr. Martin
Luther King, Jr. came to our school during the city wide school boycott
in April and he was assassinated in Memphis one week later in 1968.
Robert F. Kennedy was running for the United States presidency and
he too was assassinated in June 1968. The brothers in the BYO basically
didn't wear tailor made suits, gold watches, and diamond rings every
day and most of the members didn't drive a car. I tried my best to adjust
because I had 3 cars that were paid for, but I found myself parking my
car several blocks away from the meetings to avoid being a taxi after
our black power meetings were dismissed. July came in like a lion and

the summer was going smooth. I was working and getting ready for the summer fun with my girlfriends when I got a phone call from Sekou Sundiatta in Harlem. Sekou just said to me that "Bumpy Michaelson had died in Harlem". Sekou sounded very upset and I too was taken off guard by the sudden news. This meant, for me, that our business plans would never ever happen because I knew that you couldn't get to first base in Harlem without Bumpy Michaelson or his people being on your team. After hearing the news from Sekou Sundiatta I shifted into a deep and dark psychological depression. I started smoking excessive amounts of weed, sniffing cocaine, taking pills, and drinking cough syrup just to get high. In addition, I was having sex morning, afternoon, and night every day. My girlfriends didn't seem to mind the sexing, however, it's something about being high and having sex with your main girl. We would really come together and go straight to ecstasy and then to the stars (the wings of love). The best and most satisfying part about my sex drive was that the drugs would prolong my ejaculation and the drugs would also allow me to sex my girl all day or afternoon, and in every position imaginable. Even though the sex was great, my girlfriends were seeing a dark and ugly part of me that wasn't good or normal. My attention span was not focused on school, my attention was more focused on getting high and I would just want to have sex with my girls the second we were alone and I was erect or we were naked just lounging in my room. I didn't care, I just simply didn't give a rat's ass as to what they thought. I was still a young and strong willed 18 year old teenager and I didn't pretend to have emotional cares, only sexual needs. Diane was 2 weeks older than me and Zeva was one year younger. We were inseparable but never married. Although I adored Diane and Zeva, I continued to have affairs with other women. This led to numerous arguments with both women and they would in fact deliver physical altercations upon my other love interest. I operated as a teenager on certain underworld codes and beliefs;

For example;

If I or my 5 capos had 4 women each, we didn't interfere with the personal comings and goings of each individual family member. There are more than five million women in New York City, however, our personal women were off limits, end of discussion...#42. That's what I thought then in 1968 and what in the hell would make me think otherwise? In other words, I "love hard" as most brothers do, however, I never doubted the book, the chapter, the verse, or the code because I lived by it. I saw how violence was used in my family and my neighborhood to solve problems. The turning point had finally come for me and I knew then that I could make it on my own…if push came to shove.

It would take 10 years before a woman could unbreak my heart and that epiphany would be in the birth of my 4th daughter, Tia Tombs in 1978, and only then could I actually give up the ghost of Patrice Lumumba. First, I was determined to move on to Manhattan, and second, be a bully in my bed room with my girlfriends! I finally arrived in the city that never sleeps in 1975 on black Friday with a ready made family and the neighbors knew my name…Salute to Manhattan!

"only one thing can make a soul complete, and that thing is love"

1969

THE MICHAEL TOMBS COMPROMISE

I T WAS JULY 2, 1969. It was a little after midnight and I just left Diane Young, my girlfriend's house, headed over to Zeva's, my other girlfriend's house, to get what I came there for. We all knew I had a court appearance at 9am in the morning and sex was the best way to remove stress. As normal I broke both women off in their rooms, washed up and got into my car and drove to my friend Jimmy's house in East Orange. I smoked a couple of joints, sniffed some coke, and listened to Michael Coltrane's 'My Favorite Things" on Jimmy's living room floor. I got up around 6am locked the door and left. While driving back home I said to myself "If you're going to get lynched you might as well do it in style". I walked into my parents home about 7am and my father was dressed (suit and tie) and waiting for me, he said son "I thought you had jumped bail?" I said no dad but I need to take a bath and get washed up and put on a suit with my brown Italian alligator shoes. We headed out the door, jumped into my dad's car and drove downtown to court. When we entered Judge William Wall's court, I was surprised, because it looked like my whole neighborhood was in the court waiting for the judge to leave his chambers and take his seat on the bench. As soon as Judge William Walls took his seat on the bench, he started passing out prison sentences to everyone, including me. I was the only one in the holding cell who seemed to be in shock. I really think it's a game changer to be snatched away from other men, especially those men you look to for protection, and then placed in solitary confinement, however, that's where I found myself on July 2, 1969 and by the next morning on July 3, I was in the Essex County Penitentiary beginning a 1 to 3 year prison sentence. Just before I left home for court the morning of my sentencing I got a phone call from Sekou Sudiatta telling me that my cousin Curtis had been murdered in Harlem. In addition, I was later to be informed by Sekou that Stephanie St. Clair (Madam Queen) had passed away. Stephanie St.Clair's death was a shocking and hard hitting wake up call for me in 1969. I knew The New York City underworld was now missing major players in action and I had to accept it was now going to be a much different game plan for me in Harlem and Newark. I didn't think very much about the death of my cousin Curtis because my mind was on my trial that morning. As soon as I sat down on my bunk in my cell, I thought to myself, my cousin Curtis just got murdered in the building he lived in with my Aunt Jennifer in Harlem on 112th Street, I'm in prison in Essex County, and Sekou Sundiatta is going into a drug rehabilitation program in New York City. I didn't get any sleep that night, I just stayed awake as long as I could. I finally crashed and the next morning I was informed by the prison guards that breakfast was being served in the prison cafeteria around 6am and I got a chance to look at the prison population. At breakfast many of the stick up men and many of the bank robbers were eating at their assigned tables and I was immediately informed that I was the "youngest" brother in the prison (18 years old). Everyone knew that I was a Muslim from the "Little Bricks" in Newark, NJ as soon as I walked into the cafeteria so the cooks pointed out to me immediately what to eat and what not to eat while I was standing in line for breakfast, lunch, and diner each day until I learned the prison dietary system. Each day was the same as yesterday, preaching and teaching Islam, pumping iron, reading the al Quran, and boxing. The inmates were allowed to go to the prison yard twice a week, see a movie once a week on good behavior and all inmates were kept in lock up 23 hours every day. My father kept my prison bank account full and he took good care of my personal property and my cars. My father came to visit me every week without fail (God rest his soul, R.I.P.) and Diane and Zeva would visit twice a month. The prison was maximum security so each visit was behind a glass wall, and there was no physical contact allowed whatsoever. And the questions, by my loved ones, were always "how are you doing" and it became necessary for me to explain the same thing and give assurances that "I'm ok" each week. The weekly experience made me humble daily as I slowly began to realize that I was considered by many people and the prison staff "a convict". The inmates who would eventually serve life sentences made sure I got their pillows and blankets before they were transferred to Trenton State Prison or Rahway State Prison. All the Muslims in the prison and everyone else knew that Rubin "Hurricane" Carter was doing triple life in Trenton State Prison so many inmates were in support of exposing the legal system and having Rubin's conviction overturned and that would be by giving Rubin a new trial on his appeal. We all just had to do something, so most prisoners focused on their appeals. I didn't stay in prison very long, in fact, right after I arrived I began writing my appeal to the appellant court. In September 1969 it was granted by the Essex County appellant court, and on Thanksgiving Day November 27, 1969 I was finally released. I was reborn that day and I haven't looked back since. It was the end of my beginning. My thoughts were as I walked to freedom, "if you look backwards, you will continue to go backwards." My father was waiting for me in the visitor's area and as I was leaving the prison door, the warden said to me from inside the prison from where I was leaving, "you won't be coming back here again Michael…right?" I said "no sir." My father and I quickly went down the stairwell to the visitor's parking lot, we jumped into his car and my father drove home to Newark on Thanksgiving Day 1969. My family was excited to see me back home again (lots of hugs and kisses) and I knew they were tired of looking at my empty seat at the dinner table. My parent's apartment seemed very small when I arrived. That night after the family dinner when I lay awake and at peace with myself, when everyone was asleep, thinking about my next moves, I knew then I would be renting my own apartment soon. It was time to move out and on my own, it was high time to write a new chapter in my life. I would catch up with my girlfriends and everyone who owed me money the next day. I would later write letters to many of the prison inmates as promised, and I wrote most of my friends, and we promised to reunite whenever they were released. Some of the brothers had life sentences so I didn't see many of them for 20 years or more. I now knew what the odds were living in the ghetto and on the streets of Newark and Harlem. And I thought to myself, my security net has now been pierced. In legal terms it's called "the piercing of the veil". In the 1960s if you were charged with a crime and convicted, you most likely were going to prison if you were an African American male and not legally represented. This was long before "The Black Lives Matter Movement" "The Innocence Project" or "The New Jim Crow Movement". So the best way to keep your nose clean was to just be lucky or forget about being a player. I was later informed by Sekou Sunditta that my cousin Curtis got heavily into a drug debt uptown and wasn't willing to get with the new program in Harlem so them dope boys in Harlem sparked him right there in my aunt's hallway on 112th. My capos and their crews were chasing girls, ducking the police, and whistling past the graveyard, but them dope boys in Harlem was doing drug business, ducking the police, and visiting the graveyard everyday and very often. The heroin game had changed in Harlem and Nicky Barnes made it very clear that he had zero tolerance on how Bumpy Michaelson was running business in Harlem and he was going to run Harlem his way or else. That meant to me that the middleman had to be eliminated, and all the dominos would fall in line. In the 1970s and 1980s all underworld drug business lead to Harlem and in Harlem all roads led to Nicky Barnes and his commission. Nicky would always ask you when you first met him, "are you making money?" the answer usually was no I'm not, and Nicky would say "how could you, because we're making all the money and we own all the real estate". Nicky wasn't very comfortable with the Hollywood crowd, naturally he was north east coast, however, he would always say to the west coast crew, "if you're making so much money in Hollywood, why do you need this powder?" Leroy "Nicky" Barnes wrote in his autobiography that he loved competition, such as the famous gangsters who came to Harlem such as Frank Lucas and Goldfinger. He was also asked by a news reporter, "do you think you were a tool of the white man?" Nicky's answer was, "I probably can't answer that, but if you're into powder, you have to be vicious." "I personally think that the death of Ellesworth "Bumpy" Michaelson in 1968 and the death of Stephanie "Madam Queen" St. Clair in 1969 prompted Nicky Barnes to organize his commission similar to the Italian

"Cosa Nostra" because in my opinion Nicky Barnes psychologically believed that the teachings of "Niccolo Machiavelli" would insulate him from each gangster going for himself in Harlem." Leroy "Nicky" Barnes was the only man that I knew of who could look at you, and then look through you. If Nicky Barnes said he wanted to see you, rumor has it that your knees would begin to tremble. My capos were willing to hold the fort down in Newark while I was away in the penitentiary. They all knew they could control our neighborhood with brutal force if necessary, break a jawbone, break some guy's ribs, break both legs of a rat, or run a guy out of town with the threat of having his head blown off, or even the threat of kidnapping his family, however, they also knew they needed bosses in our neighborhood who could provide large sums of cash/or capital, like those Wall Street investors, or those hedge fund administrators with the International Monetary Fund (IMF) and that required education. According to President Richard M. Nixon in his autobiography, Nixon said, "the judgment of history depends on who writes it". According to Dr. Andrew Richardson, assistant research analyst for the Black Youth Organization, the Nicky Barnes organization at its peak in the mid 1970s was grossing 14 million dollars a year and netting 5 million dollars cash yearly. And according to Dr. Arthur Wedgewood, chief research supervising analyst for the Black Youth Organization, he noted that Guy Fisher who was caught up in the Nicky Barns sting, "Mr. Fisher finally went on trial and was found guilty, and he is now serving a life sentence in federal prison without the possibility of parole". In addition, Mr. Fisher received an undergraduate degree, a master's degree, and a PhD in sociology all while working on his clemency appeal with the federal courts. According to CBS news anchor and reporter, Walter Cronkite, the Nuremberg trials after World War 2 was a classic white boy's play book example of the German High Command trying to sell the white racist pig's lie that the "final solution" was known by only a few individuals inside the Third Reich. Walter Cronkite's research exposed that fallacy, it went on to discover that, "they knew, the entire German High Command all knew about the extermination of the Jews". There were reports of hundreds if not thousands of concentration camps all over Europe, and these camps were not universities. For example, all over occupied Europe the Germans, in fact, knew about the so called "death marches" of the Jews. The historical questions for me was, who knew, and what did they know? For example, the parents, the teachers, the doctors, the lawyers, and the judges? Even today's historians and students in colleges and universities continue to ask why didn't the Germans expose those who were guilty of these great crimes against human beings? And furthermore, how could a politician like Adolph Hitler begin a political movement that would eventually elect him and the Nazi Party to power in Germany?" The simple answer, in my opinion, was fear. The German people in the 1920s, 1930s, and 1940s had their own little petty white racist fears and Hitler was able to feed into that psychology of German thought, that was the hard reality, ultimate access, in my opinion, to German fears. Eventually Adolph Hitler made an alliance with Japan and Italy, and very soon the Japanese military felt powerful enough to bomb the United States Naval fleet at Pearl Harbor on December 7, 1941. The Japanese military attack on Pearl Harbor required the American President, Franklin D. Roosevelt, to ask the American Congress to declare war against the Empire of Japan. The United States of America officially entered the Second World War and started the difficult task of liberating Europe militarily from under Nazi control and defeating the Japanese Empire.

For example,

Many people think that society works around something called morality, in my opinion, this is a false thought process. Society actually works around something called the "law."

"People, in my opinion, who kill other people, in my opinion, eventually and irrationally recognize that killing innocent people is wrong "they can only hide the truth for so long".

DIANE YOUNG

"THE PERFECT STORM"

Introduction
Diane Young
Born September 1950-present
Other names Di, D

D IANE YOUNG IS a African American Muslim who grew up in Newark, New Jersey and graduated from East Side High School in Newark, New Jersey.

Diane Young met Michael Tombs in 1963 at Montgomery Jr. High School where we became close friends. In East Side High School Diane was outgoing and eventually became captain of the cheer leading squad at Central High School. Diane graduated from East Side High School in June 1968 and entered Essex County College in September of 1968. In 1969 she became engaged to Michael R. Tombs and the relationship was dissolved on August 18, 1970. Diane later changed her name to a Muslim name, and went on to be employed by the federal government in Newark, New Jersey. She was briefly employed at Sears & Roebuck in Newark, and finally she was employed by the United States Postal Service before retiring in 2015.

Diane is now happily married with her family.

"Where there is life there is hope, hope only disappears when you decide something is hopeless." ~Michael Tombs

Preface

First of all, although my love affair with Diane Young was a love ballad, the affair ended in Diane's betrayal of me when we were both 19 years old on August 18, 1970. As before mentioned Diane Young and I met at Montgomery Jr. High School in 1963. She had a group of young women that she hung out with and I had a group of young men that I hung out with. Our groups would sit at opposite lunch tables every day in the school cafeteria and that's how we met and became familiar. Our groups quickly paired off and I ended up with Diane and she with me. The first year was very exciting for us and I became her first boyfriend and she was my first female confidant. I would walk her home as much as I could if I didn't have to work after school. She was a member of a Methodist congregation in Newark, located on Belmont Avenue in Newark, NJ. According to Diane, she was the product of a Methodist family and we appeared to be very much in love, however, in 1964 Diane was transferred to East Side High School in Newark where she became a freshman and I remained at West Kinney Jr. High until I graduated in 1965. I entered high school as a sophomore so we both had the opportunity of enjoying our teenage years in separate high schools. That was a learning experience that would prove to be very significant during our romance in 1970. Diane was very popular, outgoing, and became captain of the cheer leading squad for East Side High School. She was beautiful, definitely gorgeous, and a target for a great date with the young men, her classmates, and the sports team members in her school and her neighborhood. I had many girlfriends at my high school and in my neighborhood so I didn't worry much about flirtations because we were growing and developing as teenagers. After we both graduated from high school and entered Essex County College, our romance began to connect on another level, this is where our love affair began to become more exclusive, my friends became her friends, and her successful goals became my successful goals. Our real test came for us both when I was sentenced to prison on July 2, 1969. That's where our romance became more focused, especially when I was released from incarceration. The point being, Diane never was independent from me, she never doubted that we could continue to grow and mature together. It was very exciting for me when I challenged Diane to grow and develop, and that's when I suggested and introduced Diane to the philosophy of The World of Islam and we began our membership The Grand Temple in Newark, NJ together to listen and to be educated by Minister Leroy Patterson. The Grand Temple is where Diane and I officially received our membership. I think at some point in her indoctrination in the MWT (Muslim women training), in my opinion, she got The World of Islam's teachings confused with the "Sunnah and the Hadiths" of al-Islam and that's where she became misinformed. In my opinion, as I reflect on this crisis, our united thought process came to an end. I didn't pretend not to be sad or devastated, however, our commonalities were now divided and now our realities were different because she was now disloyal. Diane Young took a regretful oath "blind obedience" in the World of Islam that led her to foolishly believe that she was enlightened. This regretful oath, in my opinion was irrational and unrealistic. This meant for me that it was the end of our world, the end of our age, and the end of our life as we knew it...Diane Young was never independent of me and in my final opinion on this matter, as for me, if you want to be the King or the boss, you have to pay the cost. In addition, if you don't want to pay your bills, guess what, I'm the man who will...

Betrayal and disloyalty has always been part of African American history and culture starting with America's infamous Benedict Arnold during the American Revolution. History knows and tells us in American colleges and universities that England was not defeated by the treason of Benedict Arnold. The English government in the 18th century was the most powerful military in the world. England protected China, India, and much of Africa's territory, and it was just not feasible, in my opinion, militarily to lose British soldiers as fodder in the American Revolution. In my opinion, England's military view was that the war was prosecuted by misguided American patriots believing in this "last twilight of the Gods theory."

In addition, the ideology of the American south was not defeated by the American North in the great American Civil War just because

Mary Surrat and three other male conspirators were executed for the assassination of President Abraham Lincoln. The southern government's plan to invade Mexico and institute slavery and the Confederacy's secret request to President Lincoln to join with the North, invade Canada as a Northern territory, and abolish slavery is what actually failed the southern cause, in my opinion, in the end. It was the Confederate ideology, led by Jefferson Davis in Richmond, Virginia, that was destroyed in the war effort for the southern Confederacy. Most southern capitals, including Richmond, were ordered burned and destroyed by President Lincoln and commanding General Grant, and consequently the American antebellum south was forced into a dark American era called "Reconstruction" never being fully able to emerge from the southern slavery past. This forced the Confederate surrender and the Confederate leadership to be ultimately destroyed.

"A missile can kill a terrorist, however, responsible government will kill terrorism"~ Michael R. Rice

Forward
A triple-helical structure for DNA

In the case of the molecular structure of DNA (The Double Helix) by James Watson and Francis Crick, Watson and Crick had also previously worked out a three-helical model, in 1951. But their theory was wrong. Their mistake was partly based on Watson having misremembered a talk by Rosalind Franklin where she reported that she had established the water content of DNA by using X-ray crystallographic methods. But Watson did not take notes, and remembered the numbers incorrectly. Many voices have argued that the Nobel Prize should also have been awarded to Rosalind Franklin, since her experimental data provided a very important piece of evidence leading to the solving of the DNA structure. In a recent interview in the magazine Scientific American, Watson himself suggested that it might have been a good idea to give Wilkins and Franklin the Nobel Prize in Chemistry, and him and Crick the Nobel Prize in Physiology or Medicine – in that way all four would have been honored. Rosalind Franklin died in 1958. As a rule only living persons can be nominated for the Nobel Prize, so the 1962 Nobel Prize was out of the question.

CHERYL SANCHEZ

"THE RISE, AND THE FALL, OF A MODEL"

Introduction
Cheryl Sanchez
Born 1979- present
Other names Cherry

C HERYL IS AN African American fashion designer and model who grew up in Albany, New York and graduated from high school there. Cheryl met Michael R. Tombs in 2013 when she applied for a model casting slot with Pinnacle Holdings, LLC on Facebook in 2013. During the interview process I was informed by Cheryl that she was also a gymnast and a bartender. After several subsequent interviews in Manhattan, Cheryl appeared to be a rising star in the modeling and entertainment business. In 2014 Ms. Sanchez was signed on by me as the new face of Pinnacle Holdings, LLC along with nine other models and I additionally signed Cheryl on with King Enterprises, Inc. as an Rose Street Entertainment Model. Both subsidiaries are owned by their parent company, King Enterprises, Inc. whose CEO is Michael Tombs. In May 2014 Ms. Sanchez violated her contract and I terminated the business relationship. We had no future plans to be together in show business so bank fraud was a contract/or complaint and a matter for my attorney to argue. The legal dispute was settled in court with an undisclosed agreement and Ms. Sanchez's countersuit was dismissed with prejudice. Ms. Sanchez now works as a bartender and gymnast somewhere in New York City.

Preface

"That was a confirmation in 2015 of my worst suspicions and fears".

In December of 2013 Cheryl was part of a fashion show in Harlem's Apollo Theater that featured her debut fashion line "Royalty." I wanted to support her by being there with and for her, however, I was in Miami with my public relations director making a feasibility study on transferring my women's basketball team, The Miami Fire organization from Newark to Miami. In addition, I also was working on a franchise purchase with the WNBA and my financing proposal with my hedge fund administrator was being seriously reviewed, so Cheryl and our meeting had to be postponed until the following week. Fortunately for Cheryl she got excellent radio and several local Harlem magazine reviews for her original fashion line (Royalty) and she was fully supported by her family and friends. That's what impressed me about Cheryl's business drive and determination, so I immediately set up several radio and cable TV interviews to get Cheryl promoted exclusively by King Enterprises,Inc. When I returned to Manhattan Cheryl and I were inseparable. Cheryl called me the next morning and said "I'm glad what you did to my career" I said "yeah, and I want to move forward." Cheryl and I would meet at one of our favorite Starbucks in Manhattan in the mornings or lunch at a local restaurant with my architect discussing show business, the pros and cons of a start up budget for Cheryl's fashion line (Royalty), and relocating at some time in the near future to Manhattan's east side fashion district and then on to St. Thomas (USVI) to coordinate my business plans by creating an international fashion movement that would include and collaborate with the entire Caribbean fashion and entertainment world. On June 2, 2014 Cheryl deposited a fake check into my corporate business holding account and disappeared. I was disappointed and threatened her with a legal law suit. A second check was sent to me for deposit to cover the previous transaction, however, that check was also fake. I was never given a reason or explanation why Cheryl betrayed me or why she was disloyal. I later was informed by my investigation's agency that the criminal organization Cheryl was in contact with had relocated to Connecticut and was still doing business there. I simply made a phone call to my public relations directors, and their contacts, instructing each one to send memos and alerts to Hollywood's fashion world, New York's fashion world, Chicago's fashion world, London's fashion world, Tokyo's fashion world, and Miami's fashion world to blacklist Ms. Cheryl Sanchez. In the interim, Cheryl's stardom in King Enterprises went down in flames in the Manhattan court trial. Cheryl's credibility was challenged at the discovery hearing and no one in her family, grandmother, mother, boyfriend, all were served with a personal subpoena, and no one appeared or produced any supporting evidence at any of her depositions. The discovery hearing exposed Cheryl's true purpose. She was a good amateur, a weak link, who was now up against a real professional producer (KEI). The pre-trial hearings forced the court to dismiss Cheryl's countersuit because she was unable to produce evidence to substantiate her termination counterclaim. The TV media and the civil court's mediation networks all contacted Cheryl to settle out of court, arbitrate at their office in Manhattan, or to appear on their shows. The Judge Greg Mathis Show, The People's Court with Judge Marilyn Milian, and The Hot Bench Court, all agreed to hear my case on their TV shows on network TV and Cheryl refused each request. Cheryl now knew the might of my lawsuit would eventually catch up to her. Meanwhile, my WNBA negotiations got off to a fantastic start. The WNBA president's general council requested that my holding company deposit $10 million dollars in cash for an expansion draft team and another $25 million dollars in cash to cover any other franchise fees. I requested a feasibility study in reference to why certain franchises such as, The Charlotte Sting, The Houston Comets, and The Sacramento Monarchs had cancelled their franchise agreements and why their owners and their franchises were no longer part of the WNBA play card. In addition, my holding company, Pinnacle Holdings, was financing the entire purchase via King Enterprises, Inc., so I contacted my Wells Fargo Banker to stop any automatic advance payments to any of my subsidiaries, including contractual ties to Cheryl Sanchez to avoid any overdraft fees involving the Wells Fargo Bank fraud scheme, and until my accountants over at Ernst & Young could certify the WNBA's assets.

I then made arrangements to return to Manhattan, however, all flights, trains, and buses were booked. My director of security made a personal call and reservations were made for me to take a private jet from Miami to Teterboro airport via Baltimore, Maryland into New Jersey and a private car would shuttle me home to the Archstone on west 54th in Manhattan to take control of my business crisis. Once I arrived in Manhattan I was informed through a phone call by my attorney, Gregory Powell, Esq., to immediately file a bank fraud lawsuit, The State of New York, against Cheryl Sanchez. I lost the first round, as before mentioned, in arbitration with no monetary compensation.

"I think Cheryl Sanchez just reached the end of the road"

Foreword
Excerpts From Juan Raphael The Miniseries

After the end of Reconstruction, African American, Jewish-American, Irish American, and Italian-American crime families saw a decrease in profits and decided to move in on the Harlem drug scene. Manhattan mob leaders was the first to move in, beating and killing small time drug dealers who would not pay protection.... Newark crime leaders refused to pay protection to Manhattan's crime families and commissions despite the amount of violence and intimidation by police they faced. Eventually, a negotiated truce with each family, and Newark crime leaders took over spots in Manhattan with only a percentage going to Newark. Manhattan crime leaders then had to go to Newark crime leaders first if they had any problems in Manhattan. That's when the legend of Newark began. The book "JUAN RAPHAEL THE ROAD NOT TAKEN" by Michael R. Rice, provides a factual account of this. Manhattan drug lords realized that the struggle with the Five Families was hurting their business so assassinations in 1999 on the orders of The Commissions began. Juan Raphael sent a telegram to hospital beds as the gangsters lay dying. It read, "As ye sow, so shall ye reap." The incident made headlines all around the world.

By the beginning of 2001, Juan Raphael had become the reigning business investor in East Africa while economics became the dominant business game in America. Our story begins while Juan Raphael is still rich and following the business model of the late African American "Billionaire" Reginald F. Lewis CEO of Beatrice Foods.

Poetry
The Fragrance of Light….at JUAN RAPHAEL FRAGRANCES

Our sense of smell carries deep emotional and physical triggers…. instantly transporting us to a time and place that our hearts remember even when our minds do not.

The science of healing through scent is old and wise. The Spice and Silk Routes of old date back to prehistoric times. The resins, oils and spices being transported for commerce and trade were valued beyond the gold and diamonds of these modern times.

The demands for scents and incense by the empires of antiquity, such as Egypt, Rome and Babylon, made Arabia one of the oldest trade centers of the world. The commerce of that time was plant material in every form imaginable. Empires traded and traveled on the inherent value of such sacred materials.

Today, our immediate and effortless access to such raw materials has diminished our capacity to value the incredible medicine that plant, flower, and resin oils provide for us. The old adage that familiarity breeds contempt is painfully true in this case. Oils today are denatured, bleached, adulterated, and cut with sub optimal materials. Artificial fragrances have pirated the rightful place of pure cold processed food grade anointing oils.

At JUAN RAPHAEL, a call to honor and re-ennoble the sacred plant oils of the world is absolutely part of my mission and purpose. Providing my discerning customer base with non chemicalized scent options for my formulas and products is a yoke that I enthusiastically pick up and carry.

It is with this spirit that I am so pleased to offer you one more pure plant essential oil scent blend. I call it Luminescent because it is the smell of Light itself. The extremely unique and juxtaposed notes of citrus, flower, and wood come together for a truly sublime and… dare I say…. euphoric scent.

I have sourced very particular essential oil types for this delicate perfume…in order to accommodate what I feel is a universally pleasing and healing aromatherapeutic scent.

For you!!!

Here at JUAN RAPHAEL, I am thrilled to have created a stepping stone to realize my prayer for myself and everyone and everything else. That prayer very specifically being that the light will always find me. Join me in smelling the Light. It is truly Divine!

LENA MITCHELL

"THE HONOR AND THE PLEASURE"

Introduction
Lena Mitchell
Born 1978-present
Other names Dee,

L ENA IS AN African American dancer and hair stylist who grew up in Rahway, New Jersey and Elizabeth, New Jersey. After graduating high school she moved to the Bronx, New York to live with her sister and pursue her dream career with the Dance Theater of Harlem. According to Lena, she registered in several modern dance classes at the Bronx Community College and volunteered to work at Harlem Hospital to better serve the African American community. I met Lena in the spring of 2ooo at the Dance Theater of Harlem's outreach matinee. We both enjoyed the performance and spoke about other shows we would like to see at the DTH's main theater on 152nd Street in uptown Manhattan. We exchanged phone numbers and Lena immediately noticed on my business card that I was CEO of King Enterprises, Inc. She asked me several questions about my company and I suggested we talk more about my company over lunch sometime in the near future. Lena agreed that was a much better idea and in fact called me about a month later and we met at a restaurant in the Bronx on 137th Street and Park Avenue.

Preface

The summer of 2000 came quickly and I was busy as usual, going to school, working, and making films. Lena wrote to me many serious personal inspirational letters while I was away at school. Our son Talib Q ibn was born in June of 2002.

Poetry

Rose Street Entertainment has a life time to go in the relaxation business, however, it looks like my American label is getting a bold new look, adding exciting photography to my ad campaign this fall. KEI will continue reinventing the role of my main face of my brand, contrary to rumors, while other Rose Street Models will be featured in their own published spots.

Thank you for being part of my prayers and dreams. I respect every strand in the weave that is Pinnacle Holding's manifestation. May the peace and joy fill every beautiful life on planet Earth.

PATRICIA GOMEZ

"THE PIECES OF A DREAM"

Introduction
Patricia Gomez
Born 1977- present
Other names Pat, Patty

P ATRICIA IS AN African American dancer and fashion designer who grew up in Brooklyn, New York. After graduating high school, Patricia and her best girlfriend rented a small apartment in Brooklyn's Coney Island. Patricia worked as a part time dancer in a Brooklyn strip club and worked full time as a cashier/sales Clerk for an Exxon gas station that had a grocery store. For two semesters, according to Patricia, she took courses at Medger Evers College in Brooklyn but dropped out temporarily to pay her bills. I met Patricia in December of 2002 at City Center in Manhattan where the Alvin Ailey Dance Company was performing. She was sitting right across from me and I couldn't help but notice her beauty and charm. I was a regular at the City Center when

Alvin Ailey performed in Manhattan, however, when the show began I noticed Patricia was sitting alone. At intermission I walked over and introduced myself. As we became acquainted I noticed she was very familiar with the names of the dancers performing in the show, however, she then said her date didn't show up. I sensed that she was upset so I immediately gave her my business card and to my surprise Patricia called me in the first week in January 2003.

Preface

We set a date to meet at the Brooklyn Academy of Music (BAM) about a week later. Patricia and I enjoyed the show and then we agreed to have a late night dinner to get better acquainted with each other. Patricia wrote me many personal letters of inspiration while I was away at school in Bridgeport, Connecticut. Our daughter Ashley was born in April of 2004.

Poetry

"Widely known as CEO of KEI, a NGO in New York City. Michael Tombs is also a respected entrepreneurial trailblazer. As CEO of King Enterprises, Inc. Michael grew up in New Jersey and founded his own film company through which he created Rose Street Entertainment and Pinnacle Holdings, LLC. In August 2012 Michael spoke to The Black Wall Street Alliance about the roll his NGO plays in NYC with the theme "It's time to drop that ZERO and find yourself a HERO..."

King Enterprises, Inc. is twenty-two years (1994) into the art of cable TV and film productions. Through refined tweaking and stretching and growing, KEI continues to shine like a beacon in the night amidst subpar uninspired industry competitors. KEI knows exactly what your needs are. Just like you my sensitive and honest pulse on life, as dynamic as it is, is part of what makes KEI so dam good at giving you exactly what works for today's discerning consumer. Whether its massage therapy, fragrances and body essentials THE ROAD NOT TAKEN is branded! At KEI I'm always aware of you, without you, I do not exist. You give me purpose and meaning and direction and value in my professional endeavors. I continue to strive to be the most effective, elegant, affordable production company in the world.

Bless you and thank you for giving me so many reasons to try harder, do better, and create as much beauty as I can each and every single week.

May the Light always find you in every moment. Aquarius Productions, Inc, remains faithfully in service to you, our customers, our community, and our planet.

MY AFTER THOUGHTS
AND CONGO
REFLECTIONS

THIS SACRED LIFE is an endless opportunity to give and receive love. I'm asked by Life to go deeper, to care more, to find a better way to express the love that I'm all about. I'm challenged to grow in faith and consciousness as great uncertainty looms in every moment of my existence. I understand that you choose to invest in my product for your fragrances and body essentials because I'm making the same prayer that you are. The prayer is this…more life and more love for everyone please. My narrative and philosophy is endlessly reaching for new ways of doing what I do that honor and support more life and more love for all of life.

The ingredients that I choose, the people that I employ, the practices that I take on and cast aside, what I decide to value, the intention that I infuse into my work culture, the words that I choose, the risks that I take, the respect that I practice with my women, daughters, and sons…, it all adds up to the prayer that I'm attempting to live.

Thank you for caring about this with me. It's a better prayer with you in it.

May all of life be honored and cherished. May there be peace for all. May all be loved.

May everyone and everything eat and sleep and have water and be safe from harm.

May this special season and these special years be the next most necessary opportunity to express more love to your people, places, and things.

May this special season and these special years be the next most necessary time to receive more love from your people, places, and things.

WHAT GOES AROUND

(ENLIGHTENMENT)

G EORGE WASHINGTON WILLIAMS,
"An Open Letter to His Serene Majesty
Leopold II, King of the Belgians and Sovereign of the Independent State
of Congo By Colonel, The Honorable Geo. W. Williams, of the United
States of America," 1890

Good and Great Friend,

I have the honor to submit for your Majesty's consideration some
reflections respecting the Independent State of Congo, based upon
a careful study and inspection of the country and character of the
personal Government you have established upon the African Continent.

It afforded me great pleasure to avail myself of the opportunity
afforded me last year, of visiting your State in Africa; and how
thoroughly I have been disenchanted, disappointed and disheartened,
it is now my painful duty to make known to your Majesty in plain but
respectful language. Every charge which I am about to bring against

your Majesty's personal Government in the Congo has been carefully investigated; a list of competent and veracious witnesses, documents, letters, official records and data has been faithfully prepared, which will be deposited with Her Britannic Majesty's Secretary of State for Foreign Affairs, until such time as an International Commission can be created with power to send for persons and papers, to administer oaths, and attest the truth or falsity of these charges.

There were instances in which Mr. HENRY M. STANLEY sent one white man, with four or five Zanzibar soldiers, to make treaties with native chiefs. The staple argument was that the white man's heart had grown sick of the wars and rumors of war between one chief and another, between one village and another; that the white man was at peace with his black brother, and desired to "confederate all African tribes" for the general defense and public welfare. All the sleight-of-hand tricks had been carefully rehearsed, and he was now ready for his work. A number of electric batteries had been purchased in London, and when attached to the arm under the coat, communicated with a band of ribbon which passed over the palm of the white brother's hand, and when he gave the black brother a cordial grasp of the hand the black brother was greatly surprised to find his white brother so strong, that he nearly knocked him off his feet in giving him the hand of fellowship. When the native inquired about the disparity of strength between himself and his white brother, he was told that the white man could pull up trees and perform the most prodigious feats of strength. Next came the lens act. The white brother took from his pocket a cigar, carelessly bit off the end, held up his glass to the sun and complaisantly smoked his cigar to the great amazement and terror of his black brother. The white man explained his intimate relation to the sun, and declared that if he were to request him to burn up his black brother's village it would be done. The third act was the gun trick. The white man took a percussion cap gun, tore the end of the paper, which held the powder to the bullet, and poured the powder and paper into the gun, at the same time slipping the bullet into the sleeve of the left arm. A cap was placed upon the nipple of the gun, and the black brother was implored to step off ten yards and shoot at his white brother to demonstrate his statement that he was a spirit, and, therefore, could not be killed. After much begging the black brother aims the gun at his white brother, pulls the trigger, the gun is discharged, the white man stoops . . . and takes the bullet from his shoe!

By such means as these, too silly and disgusting to mention, and a few boxes of gin, whole villages have been signed away to your Majesty.

When I arrived in the Congo, I naturally sought for the results of the brilliant programme: "fostering care", "benevolent enterprise", an "honest and practical effort" to increase the knowledge of the natives "and secure their welfare". 1 had never been able to conceive of Europeans, establishing a government in a tropical country, without building a hospital; and yet from the mouth of the Congo River to its head-waters, here at the seventh cataract, a distance of 1,448 miles, there is not a solitary hospital for Europeans, and only three sheds for sick Africans in the service of the State, not fit to be occupied by a horse. Sick sailors frequently die on board their vessels at Banana Point; and if it were not for the humanity of the Dutch Trading Company at that place–who has often opened their private hospital to the sick of other countries–many more might die. There is not a single chaplain in the employ of your Majesty's Government to console the sick or bury the dead. Your white men sicken and die in their quarters or on the caravan road, and seldom have Christian burial. With few exceptions, the surgeons of your Majesty's Government have been gentlemen of professional ability, devoted to duty, but usually left with few medical stores and no quarters in which to treat their patients. The African soldiers and laborers of your Majesty's Government fare worse than the whites, because they have poorer quarters, quite as bad as those of the natives; and in the sheds, called hospitals, they languish upon a bed of bamboo poles without blankets, pillows or any food different from that served to them when well, rice and fish.

I was anxious to see to what extent the natives had "adopted the fostering care" of your Majesty's "benevolent enterprise" (?), and I was doomed to bitter disappointment. Instead of the natives of the Congo "adopting the fostering care" of your Majesty's Government, they everywhere complain that their land has been taken from them by force; that the Government is cruel and arbitrary, and declare that they neither love nor respect the Government and its flag. Your Majesty's Government has sequestered their land, burned their towns, stolen their property, enslaved their women and children, and committed other crimes too numerous to mention in detail. It is natural that they everywhere shrink from "the fostering care" your Majesty's Government so eagerly proffers them.

There has been, to my absolute knowledge, no "honest and practical effort made to increase their knowledge and secure their welfare." Your Majesty's Government has never spent one franc for educational purposes, nor instituted any practical system of industrialism. Indeed the most unpractical measures have been adopted against the natives in nearly every respect; and in the capital of your Majesty's Government at Boma there is not a native employed. The labor system is radically unpractical; the soldiers and laborers of your Majesty's Government are very largely imported from Zanzibar at a cost of £10 per capita, and from Sierra Leone, Liberia, Accra and Lagos at from £1 to £1/10 per capita. These recruits are transported under circumstances more cruel than cattle in European countries. They eat their rice twice a day by the use of their fingers; they often thirst for water when the season is dry; they are exposed to the heat and rain, and sleep upon the damp and filthy decks of the vessels often so closely crowded as to lie in human ordure. And, of course, many die.

Upon the arrival of the survivors in the Congo they are set to work as laborers at one shilling a day; as soldiers they are promised sixteen shillings per month, in English money, but are usually paid off in cheap handkerchiefs and poisonous gin. The cruel and unjust treatment, to which these people are subjected breaks the spirits of many of them, makes them distrust and despise your Majesty's Government. They are enemies, not patriots.

There are from sixty to seventy officers of the Belgian army in the service of your Majesty's Government in the Congo of whom only about thirty are at their post; the other half are in Belgium on furlough. These officers draw double pay—as soldiers and as civilians. It is not my duty to criticize the unlawful and unconstitutional use of these officers coming into the service of this African State. Such criticism will come with more grace from some Belgian statesman, who may remember that there is no constitutional or organic relation subsisting between his Government and the purely personal and absolute monarchy your Majesty has established in Africa. But I take the liberty to say that many of these officers are too young and inexperienced to be entrusted with the difficult work of dealing with native races. They are ignorant of native character, lack wisdom, justice, fortitude and patience. They have estranged the natives from your Majesty's Government, have sown the seed of discord between tribes and villages, and some of them have stained the uniform of the Belgian officer with murder, arson and robbery. Other officers have served the State faithfully, and deserve well of their Royal Master.

From these general observations I wish now to pass to specific charges against your Majesty's Government.

A SONG FOR MICHAEL TOMBS

(CRITIQUE OF JUDGMENT)

R EVEREND WILLIAM HENRY Sheppard (1865–1927) was one of the earliest African Americans to become a missionary for the Presbyterian Church. He spent 20 years in Africa, primarily in and around the Congo Free State, and is best known for his efforts to publicize the atrocities committed against the Kuba Kingdom and other Congolese peoples by King Leopold II's Force Publique. Sheppard's efforts contributed to the contemporary debate on European colonialism and imperialism in the region, particularly amongst those of the African American community. However, it has been noted that he traditionally received little attention in literature on the subject.

Early life

Sheppard was born in Waynesboro, Virginia on March 8, 1865, to William Henry Sheppard, Sr. and Fannie Frances Sheppard (née Martin), a free "dark mulatto", a month before the end of the American Civil War. No records exist to confirm William Sr.'s status as a slave or freedman, but it has been speculated that he may have been among the slaves forced to serve the Confederacy as Union troops marched upon the South. William Sr. was a barber, and the family has been described as the closest to middle class that blacks could have achieved given the time and place. At age twelve, William Jr. became a stable boy for a white family several miles away while continuing to attend school; he remembered his two-year stay fondly and maintained written correspondence with the family for many years. Sheppard next worked as a waiter to put himself through the newly created Hampton Institute, where Booker T. Washington was among his instructors in a program that allowed students to work during the day and attend classes at night. A significant influence on his appreciation for native cultures was the "Curiosity Room", in which the school's founder maintained a collection of Native Hawaiian and Native American works of art. Later in life he would collect artifacts from the Congo, specifically those of the Kuba, and bring them back for this room, as evidenced by his letters home, such as "[i]t was on the first of September, 1890 that William H. Sheppard addressed a letter to General Samuel Armstrong, Hampton, From Stanley Pool, Africa, that he had many artifacts, spears, idols, etc., and he was '...saving them for the Curiosity Room at Hampton'".

After graduation, Sheppard was recommended to Tuscaloosa Theological Institute (now Stillman College, which dedicated its library in Sheppard's honor in 1959) in Alabama. He met Lucy Gantt near the end of his time there and the two became engaged, although they would not marry for ten years. Sheppard cultivated a desire to preach in Africa, but despite the support of Tuscaloosa founder Charles Stillman, the Southern Presbyterian Church had yet to establish its mission in the Congo. He was ordained in 1888 and served as pastor to a church in Atlanta, Georgia, but did not adapt well to the life of an urban black in a heavily segregated area of the Southern United States. After two years of writing to the Presbyterian Foreign Missionary Board in Baltimore, Maryland to inquire about starting a mission in Africa, he became frustrated by the vague rationale of the rejection letters and took a train to Baltimore to ask the chairman in person. The man politely informed Sheppard that the board would not send a black man without a white supervisor.

Samuel Lapsley, an eager but inexperienced white man from a wealthy family, finally enabled Sheppard's journey to Africa. They "inaugurated the unique principle of sending out together, with equal ecclesiastical rights and, as far as possible, in equal numbers, white and colored workers".

THE HUMAN GROWTH
OF MICHAEL TOMBS

Midnight, Crescent,Royalty
"The new fragrances for Women"

STEP 1

M Y FRAGRANCES & BODY ESSENTIALS is running on all cylinders as your personal care orders come pouring into my magical manufacturing facility at THE ARCHSTONE in Manhattan. My elves are working around the clock to give it to you in the best way ever...... just how you like it to be. So visit me...

Quality, efficiency, ingenuity, sustainability and love are infused into each and every particle of your lotions, creams, oils and fragrances. Ultimately, it is our Mother Earth who we turn to in thanks and gratitude for all that she gives every single day. From her bountiful and benevolent body, we take and harvest and plow and grow in order to have industry for our lives and support for our very human experience. At KEI, I strive to honor her perfect brilliance in every raw material which graces our lives and business. It is from this intention and attention that the excellence of my formulas occurs. Please take time to remember her, and thank her for mothering my economic dream, and never forget to pass my DVD series on by being generous and thoughtfull.

Thank you for being part of my prayers and dreams. I respect every strand in the weave that is Michael Tombs's manifestation. May the peace and joy fill every beautiful life on planet Earth.

Dice & Cruise
"The new fragrances for Men"

STEP 2
Many skincare enthusiasts are just now becoming aware of what I have been honoring for many years.

Known as the King of Carotenoids and the Queen of Antioxidants, Astaxanthin is unquestioningly the reigning champion of youthening skingredients.

Astaxanthin is a very unique algae that turns red as it begins to synthesize. Its ORAC value.....Oxygen Radical Absorption Capacity... is 550 times stronger than the purest forms of vitamin E. You read that right!!!! This is serious skin repair business.

These off the charts ORAC ratings translate into a turbo powered free radical scavenger that cannot be outdone by the harshest or most extreme skin pollutants on this planet.

WOW! Simply wow! Can you appreciate why I find every excuse possible to add Astaxanthin to our daily formulating repertoires?!

Astaxanthin is grown in and harvested from fresh water sources. Once it is turned into a liquid, it becomes THE MOST IMPORTANT nutrient known to the natural world. It is what gives Salmon their red coloring and it is exactly what makes it possible for them to swim upstream and jump UP waterfalls for weeks. Astaxanthin turns Salmon into superheroes.

Astaxanthin is a fat soluble phytochemical rich antioxidant that is able to permeate cells and tissues in a unique way. Water soluble antioxidants and nutrients cannot penetrate the same blood barriers that fat soluble nutrients can. Thus Astaxanthin is absorbed deeply and richly into the dermal matrix for immediate rejuvenation, cellular growth and healing.

Skin damage and repair happens immediately when Astaxanthin is present. Dermal tone, texture, resiliency, clarity, and fullness are immediately enhanced and supported. Long term use of Astanxanthin results in visibly noticeable results.

Astaxanthin will imbue every formula that it is used in with a clear bright orange hue. This is normal and part of its cosmetic charm. It is an ACTIVE and ALIVE nutrient that knows its way around your biology. Your skin will quite literally eat it up and be the better for it.

STEP 3
KERATIN CONDITIONER
Keratin and hair have historically shown themselves to be symbiotic in bringing out each other's best qualities. As hair becomes tired and worn out from the relentless tease spray scorch paradigm…..rebuilding the hair shaft becomes unquestionably necessary and relevant. Even hair that is spared of color, curling and hairdryers is still at the brunt of the oxidizing suns rays, the drying impact of forced heat and cool air, and the solvent rich world of shampoos and chemicals. Thus, hair repair is always an excellent idea.

Keratin Conditioner is a concentrated delivery system of healing oils, botanicals, amino acids, and Keratin…….for hair that becomes you.

STEP 4
Luxurious Shampoo
Michael Tombs has been crystal clear about true beauty since 2004. It is deeply understood that living breathing thinking and feeling bodies blossom and bloom when high integrity materials from nature's pharmacy are introduced into their biosphere.

Which is precisely why my hair care products are necessary ingredients of living nutrition and nourishment for your living locks. Anemic hair is a sad situation. Hungry hair syndrome is marked by difficult, unmanageable, limp, lusterless, flat and splitting hair. The solution is to feed your hair and feed it well.

Hair longs for silica, raw lipids, keratin, and herbs for a healthy scalp. Hair needs vitamins and minerals and gentle detoxification that will not leave it stripped.

My Shampoo is just the eco-friendly, sustainable nourishing rich meal that your hair wants and deserves. This new formula is noticeably saturated with wild herbs and berries. Luxurious lipids such as Argan oil, Broccoli Seed oil, and a Passionflower Oil lubricate formula for shining results. Vitamins and Aloe Vera soothe and support the inherent flexibility and movement of your hair. This beautiful formula is gentle and suitable for daily use for all ages and all hair types and textures. I intend to make your life better and easier, and this hair repair cleanser is one easy and beautiful step in that direction. The end result of using this product is bouncy, silky, flowing and sexy healthy hair. This brand new body essential will be sold exclusively at my flag ship store in Manhattan only.

STEP 5
Wash and Anoint Biologique
The days of "Lye and Suds" have come and gone. We now know enough to respect the critical ph balance of our skins acid mantle. When protected and nurtured rather than scrubbed and stripped, skin is able to defend itself from bacteria and an ever compromised environment. Soaps in any form strip the skin of this protection as well as stripping the natural sebum and oils from the skins surface. The end result is skin that ages prematurely, is wrinkled and dry, loses its bounce and stretch, develops the dreaded crepe skin of our vanity nightmares….and ultimately lacks the health or resilience that we desire.

Enter stage left…..Wash and Anoint Body Cleansing Oil Biologique. A multi action body cleanser and healing treatment. Made for daily use. The oils are luxurious and rich. Nature based cold pressed plant oils lend antioxidants, lipids, polyphenols, and receivable vitamins and minerals for hungry skin to be fed and worshipped. It's a beautiful thing!

OBBO Wash and Anoint Body Cleansing Oil
The unique blend of oils and natural plant surfactants as well as disinfecting and healing essential oils create a wonderful biome for your skin.

To use: Spread over wet skin in the shower or bath as you would a gel or bar soap. Massage into limbs, trunk, parts and pits…then rinse.
That's it.

Not only is your skin clean, fresh, plump and glowing…..it is also moisturized and sealed …making additional lotion or cream unnecessary. The convenience of this alone has made me slightly obsessed with this new and very old way of washing and anointing the temples that we live in.

Lightning Source UK Ltd.
Milton Keynes UK
UKHW010952231122
412703UK00001B/112

9 781514 451250